25 Dog (

Step by Step Instructions for a Variety of Obedience Commands and Tricks to Teach Your Dog

By Brandon Burke

Table of Contents

Introduction

Almost every pet owner appreciates the place of a dog in the family. Dogs are greatly admired for their affection, loyalty and playful enthusiasm not to mention that they are also good when it comes to protection. When dealing with your dog however, it is important to understand that they are very different from human beings and other animals as well. Though loyal and innocent, dogs have some annoying tendencies that can make life difficult for you as the owner when living with them.

However, dogs can also be trained to help enhance their relationship with the owner while at the same time making life harmonious whenever they are. Learning the best dog training skills will help improve the bond between you and your dog and make the environment safer for all. Dogs are amazing in that they are capable of learning new lessons and commands and the most important thing therefore, is to understand how to communicate with them. Your dog will greatly change its behavior if properly trained, and complying with your instructions will never be a daunting task if the initial training is done properly.

With this in mind, it is important to understand that training a dog new tricks and commands is an art that should be approached carefully if you are to succeed. There are many arguments as to how training should be done, but the most important approach is to always make sure that you assert yourself as the dominant leader during the training. Dogs can be naughty sometimes, and yet very obedient at other times, and both behaviors must be dealt with appropriately. You will need to learn how to punish a dog for any naughty behavior, while at the same time rewarding the good behavior it exhibits. However, always remember that training your dog is all about influence and not domination. Trying to dominate your dog could backfire on you badly, but seeking to influence "man's best friend" will work amazingly during and after the training.

This book will avail very useful information to help you master the art of training your dog new tricks and commands, and at the end of it all, you will appreciate the new responses you see in your canine friend. Here, we will concentrate on the top 25 things that your dog should be trained on, and guide you on exactly how to do it.

Chapter 1: SIT

This is normally one of the first and most important commands that every dog should be taught. It is not a difficult command and the most important factor during the training is to have your dog capture the word and associate it with the related action. Once your dog has learned this command, the groundwork will always be set for other commands such as "stay" and "down".

How to do it

Required time: This command should be done for 5 to 10 minutes at a time, and it is good to repeat it at least 2 to 3 times every day until your dog catches on. Consistency is very important in this.

I.   First of all, capture your dog's attention and let it see that you have a treat ready in your hand.

II. Once you have your dog's attention, hold the treat a few inches above its nose. Avoid holding it too high as this could encourage the dog to jump.

III. Move the treat backwards such that the dog will follow it with the eyes and nose while bending backwards. This will automatically see your dog sit down as the snout looks up towards the treat.

IV. Remove the treat from that position, then follow the same process but this time call out your dog's name, and then say "sit" firmly and clearly. Once your dog is in a sitting position, say "yes" (or "good girl", etc.) and give the treat to it as you stroke and pat its back.

V. With time, start issuing the "sit" command without holding the treat close to the nose. You can move your hand gradually and say "sit". If your dog sits down, audibly say, "Good sit" and then give him/her the treat.

VI. Gradually, stop using the hand gesture or keeping the treat nearby. Instead, just say, "sit" and if your dog obeys the command, appreciate his/her obedience verbally and then give the treat.

VII. Repeat this 3 to 5 times each day until your dog catches on, and then try it out once a day for a while to make sure he/she remembers, until you finally feel that the command is thoroughly engrained.

Advice

You should use your dog's favorite food as the treat. This could be in form of cheese, chicken, salami, fish skin, or ham.

Chapter 2: COME

This is an important behavioral and safety command that your dog should learn. The command should be practiced until you are absolutely sure that the dog will obey it before letting him/her loose where safety is at stake (ex: imagine your dog is in the middle of a road, and you see a car coming so you want him/her to "come" to get out of harm's way).

How to do it

I. Put your dog on leash and hold the end of it.

II. When the dog is not paying attention, call her name and then say, "come" and make a gesture or start moving backwards.

III. If the dog responds and comes to you, give it a treat but avoid being overexcited.

IV. In case the dog doesn't respond to the command, pull the leash lightly as a way of encouraging him. Keep a cheerful, thrilled tone when issuing the command to communicate that "come" is a positive thing.

V. Once your dog starts responding when you tug the leash, try removing it and repeat the "come" command to train response without any form of manipulation.

VI. Repeat this same procedure 5 or 6 times every day until your dog has mastered it fully.

Advice

- Never use a harsh tone when issuing the "come" command, and don't use this command at all to call the dog for negative things such as pills and punishments. Doing so will cause the dog to associate the command with negative things and thus might not respond.
- Use treats carefully and infrequently to avoid over-reliance. Your dog might never respond if it does not see a treat readily available and this might affect its obedience especially during emergencies.

Chapter 3: STAY

The stay command is very important especially when preventing a dog from engaging in a dangerous situation. It can also help keep your dog calm especially when in public places. You should spend approximately 2 to 3 sessions per day, each broken into 5 to 10 minutes to train this command.

How to do it

I.   Put a leash and a collar on the dog and instruct his/her to sit.

II.   Once the dog has sat down, appreciate her by stroking or patting his/her back and if possible, avoid using a treat.

III. Hold your hand up with the palm out and then issue a firm and clear order with the word "stay".

IV.   If your dog stays motionless for 2 to 5 seconds, say "good stay" in a cheerful tone and then give him/her a treat.

V.   Encourage your dog to move a bit and them call his/her name and repeat the motion and command again. Step back and if your dog stays in the same position for a few seconds, say "good stay" and give her a treat. If he/she moves, repeat the "sit" command and then issue the "stay" command. Appreciate obedience and give a treat if the dog obeys.

VI. Say "okay" or "come" to release the dog and encourage her to move.

VII. Repeat the process at least 5 to 6 times each day and with time reduce the use of your hands and gradually prolong the duration between the "stay" and "okay" commands.

Advice

- With time, seek to increase the distance between you and your dog, but remain visible until he/she masters the command.

- As the dog obeys the command constantly, try to issue the same with distractions. This could be in form of movements a few meters away from the dog. If he/she masters the command while there are distractions, reward the obedience with a treat.

Chapter 4: WAIT

Training your dog to wait is important as it will help keep your dog safe or discipline it in such a way that it can stay in one place even in moments of distraction. The "wait" command tells the dog not to move until you give permission.

How to do it

I. Put your dog on a short leash and walk him/her to your front door. The leash gives you control over your dog especially before it understands the "wait" command.

II. Start by giving your dog a "STAY" or "SIT" command to help it remain still for long. Once the dog is in a sitting or a stay position, slightly open the door for you to get outside leaving the dog inside the house.

III. The next thing is that your dog will want to join you outside and thus might try to open the door. Through an opening, raise your palm up for the dog to see and clearly say, "WAIT".

IV. If your dog doesn't wait, hold the leash firmly to stop it from moving and close the door but don't be disappointed.

V. Repeat the second step and see how your dog behaves. You can also try this command in a different way and put your dog's favorite food nearby. Your dog will try to go towards the food. Issue the "SIT" or "STAY" command and once the dog is in this position, release the leash a bit and as your dog starts to move slightly, raise your palm and issue a "WAIT" command.

VI.   If the dog doesn't obey the command, hold the leash firmly to stop him/her. If she obeys the command, clearly say "OKAY" and release him/her to be free.

VII.   Practice this command for 5-10 minutes and do it at least 4-5 times every day. Do not extend the training sessions otherwise, your dog might not concentrate for long.

Chapter 5: LIE DOWN

This command helps in different ways and can help deal with different unwanted behaviors. Training your dog to lie down will help deal with common behaviors such as surfing counters or jumping up irritably. It also helps when riding in the car and you want your dog to be safer by maintaining more contact with the seat and a lower center of gravity.

How to do it

I.   Have a treat in your hand and then seek your dog's attention.

II.   Have your dog sit down and then move the treat towards the ground slowly accompanied by a firm and clearly spoken "DOWN" command.

III. Your dog will start moving towards the ground but motivated more by the treat. In an upbeat tone, give it a "LIE DOWN" or simply "DOWN" command.

IV.   Once the dog lies down, praise her by saying "GOOD" or "OKAY", pat his/her head, and give the treat.

V.   Seek to train the dog indoors, outdoors and under different conditions to master the command fully.

Advice

If your dog doesn't lie down, avoid pushing him/her or pinning him/her to the ground. Repeat the training steps above throughout the day and try using different treats especially those which are your dog's favorite.

Chapter 6: KISS

Most if not all dogs like kissing as a part of their social behavior. This therefore can be one of the easiest commands to train your dog at any given time.

How to do it

I.   Have cream cheese or peanut butter at hand. Place a small amount on your cheek or any other part of the body such as the hand.

II. Lean towards your dog and with a clear, upbeat tone give a "KISS" command to your dog as you point to the dab.

III. Your dog will gladly lick the cream cheese or peanut butter. Practice this several times each day and at times do it without using the yummy treats.

Advice

In case your dog becomes overly exuberant, you can also come up with a "stop kissing" command. However, avoid saying "STOP KISSING" and instead use "STOP" or ENOUGH" to communicate with your dog.

Chapter 7: OFF

The off command is necessary when seeking to stop your dog from doing something like climbing on the sofa, countertop, our guest's leg, or your bed. When embarking on the command, it is important to know that this is very different from the previously commands discussed above.

How to do it

I. Wait until the moment when your dog jumps onto something or when she starts behaving inappropriately before giving out the "OFF "command.

II. As you issue the command, you can use a treat and direct the dog towards the same. Do not use a treat without issuing a firm "OFF" command as this could easily confuse the dog without getting the desired results.

III. Continue with this same procedure each time your dog jumps on people or climbs to the sofa until it masters the lesson fully.

IV. As you continue, issue the command without giving a treat. Your dog can easily become dependent on treats thus making obedience cosmetic rather than real. Instead of issuing the command with a treat at hand, only give the treat after your dog has obeyed the "OFF" command. Also, you can use your friendly, kind, sweet-toned voice as a "treat" of sorts too. So, as soon as your dog has obeyed your firm command, just say in your loving voice "GOOD GIRL!" OR "GOOD BOY!" That way your dog becomes less reliant on salami and instead simply more content to please you.

Chapter 8: LEAVE IT

This command is intended to prevent a dog from picking unwanted things up. Your dog might try to play with your children's toys or bring in litter from outside. You can stop this untoward behavior using the "leave it" command.

How to do it

I. When teaching the "leave it" command, it is important to show your dog that leaving what you are telling him/her to do could result to a greater thing or reward. You should therefore have a treat ready and show it to him/her.

II. As your dog picks or engages in an inappropriate thing or behavior, issue a clear "leave it" command and if it leaves what it was doing, pat it and praise him/her before giving the treat.

III. Your dog should have the leash on and if it does not obey the command, you should pull the leash gently to draw him/her away from the thing or place you want it to leave.

IV. Exercise the command a few times each day until your dog has fully understood even in absence of a treat.

V. Never give the treat to your dog before it obeys you otherwise, it might not easily understand the "leave it" command.

Advice

Clapping your hands, slapping a rolled up newspaper against your own leg, or some other version of obnoxious noise is often a good deterrent that can accompany the "leave it" command, especially at first during the training. Later on, once your dog understands the command you won't need to make any other noise at all.

Chapter 9: HEEL

The most important thing when training your dog to heel is to get his attention. Training your dog the "heel" command requires firmness and consistency. Heeling is not that easy for the dog to master. It means that your dog will stay close to your left leg (or right leg if that's what you choose) until you release him/her. You should do a lot of repetitions but don't expect results as fast as you would in the other basic commands.

How to do it

I. First, heel command can be trained with a leash on or off your dog. The leash should however be used for security purposes only and not to force your dog to remain in your desired position.

II. Let your dog stand next to your left leg as you face the same direction with him/her.

III. Hold a treat near your waist but not directly close to the dog's nose. Call your dog's name to get her attention before moving two or three steps forward and then stop. If your dog is in a heel position (right next to your leg), pat him/her and then give the treat.

IV. Once your dog has finished with the treat, repeat the second and third step and stop again. Each time your dog responds positively, praise, pat and give him/her a treat. Only give the treat when the dog is in a heel position and not as a lure or bribe.

21

V. If your dog lurks behind or goes ahead of you, say "no-no-no" in disapproval but don't be too harsh. Repeat the steps above until your dog show some positive responses.

VI. Next, start walking a longer distance with your dog next to your left leg, stop, and as your dog responds, give him/her a reward.

VII. Repeat the training for 5-10 minutes, 4-5 times every day.

Chapter 10: GO TO BED

Learning the "go to bed" command is very important as it will help prevent your dog from becoming a nuisance especially when you have important chores or guests to attend to. By sending your dog to his/her place, you will be able to enjoy peace while avoiding unnecessary disturbances in your home.

How to do it

I. Set your dog's sleeping area prior to the training. This could be in one corner of your house or in a crate. Make sure the place is comfortable enough for your canine.

II. Have your dog on leash and with a treat in hand, call him/her name to capture its attention followed by "go to bed" command. As you give this command, lead your dog towards the bed and repeat the command again.

III. If in a kennel or on a bed, your dog will likely enter there and stand. Issue the "down" and "stay" commands. Once your dog goes down, praise him/her and give the reward. Don't praise your dog so much as doing so could make him/her too excited and think that you are playing.

IV. In case your dog gets up too soon, say "NO" clearly yet in an upbeat tone and then repeat the steps above again and again.

V.   As with all other commands, your "go to bed" command or training should be repeated a few times every day to help your dog understand what is required.

Chapter 11: BRING

Fetch and bring command is an amazing game you can play with your dog. Giving your dog this kind of training could help use the skills when you need to send him/her to bring something to you when performing certain chores. Or it could just be used for a fun game of fetch in the park.

How to do it

I. The first thing will be to have your dog show interest in a ball or an object. Once he/she does this, give your dog a treat and praise.

II. To begin with, give your dog a sit command and once she is attentively in position, throw the ball or whatever object you are using and once she has it in the mouth, give a "come" command. Once the dog comes to you, you can proceed by issuing a clear "bring" command in an upbeat tone.

III. If your dog picks the ball or the object in his/her mouth, give a "bring it" command. Your dog will not respond automatically and this has to be repeated a number of times. Luckily, your dog will likely naturally eventually bring it to you because otherwise, the game of fetch stops, and your dog doesn't want that. However, you want it to associate the "bring" command with the action, so once the dog has brought the ball to you, pat, praise and give a reward.

Advice

- Don't engage your dog in a chase game when training the "bring it" command. Doing so will excite the dog making her think you want to play.

- Try using a leash if your dog persistently doesn't want to bring the ball to you. Throw the ball a few meters away and once your dog has the ball, issue the "come" command. If he/she doesn't bring the ball, pull the leash a bit to direct the dog towards you.

- Be very still, and only stick out your hand but don't lean or move your arm too forward towards your dog, especially further into the training. This way, your dog will learn that it needs to bring the ball and put it all the way in the palm of your hand. Before you know it, the game will be super fun for your dog, meanwhile entirely effortless for you.

Chapter 12: DROP IT

The "drop it' training can be of help especially when you want your dog to let go off something in his mouth. This training is very important especially in dealing with emergency issues or when dealing with issues requiring protection. It can also help during games, such as fetch, so that you don't end up playing tug-of-war each time your dog brings the toy back.

How to do it

I.   Use your dog's favorite toy or a ball and drop it on the ground. Follow this by issuing a "take it" command and once this happens, pat and praise your dog. This can help train your dog how to pick something fast before doing the "drop it" part.

II.   Once it is in the mouth, issue a "drop it" or "drop" command firmly and clearly with your hand motioning him/her towards the ground.

III.   As soon as she drops the ball or the toy, give him/her a treat.

IV.   In case your dog doesn't drop the ball or the toy, try holding or waving the treat next to his/her nose but do not try to wrestle or pull the ball or toy from the mouth. Doing so will give your dog the wrong signal which can be interpreted as punishment or a game.

V.   Repeat the process numerous times each day giving a treat to your dog whenever it obeys the orders.

VI. As your dog masters the right response, start withdrawing the treat to prevent any reliance on the same.

Advice

You can use other words such as "give" or "release" to teach this trick if you prefer that over "drop". Additionally, leashes can be used on dogs that are very playful as a way of containing them during the training.

Chapter 13: BACK UP

Back up can be a fun trick to train your dog. It is very helpful especially when you want to keep your dog from dashing through an open door or space or if he is crowding you when you want to attend to some serious matters. You will need treats and patience when training your dog this trick.

How to do it

I. To begin with, your dog needs to have been given the "stay" command training. If this has been done, give him/her a stay command to help capture his/her attention.

II. Stand facing your dog from a few meters away.

III. Using your hand to motion your dog, give the "back up" command and then start moving towards the dog. Some dogs might not move at all while others will take a few steps away from you as you draw closer.

IV. If your dog doesn't move an inch when you draw closer, keep moving towards and attempt to lean forward a little. This might force your dog to move backward a bit and once this happens, tell him/her "good" and then give a treat.

V. Practice this for about 5 sessions each taking ten minutes and soon your dog will know and respond to your commands.

Advice

- In case your dog doesn't step back when you issue the "back up" command, try encouraging him/her and use hand motions all the time.
- You can also use your body especially the leg to push the dog backwards but this should be done gently.

Chapter 14: SHAKE PAWS

It can be an amazing thing to have your dog offering her paws to visitors when they come over. This trick is not difficult to train but will leave your visitors impressed always.

How to do it

I. Command your dog to sit down and hold your dog's favorite treat in a clasped hand. Your dog should see the treat but not get it until she responds to your command in a positive way.

II. Call your dog's name and give the "shake" command while waving the clasped fist under her nose. This arouses interest in the dog and he/she will start sniffing at the hand hoping to get the treat, and eventually will begin pawing at your hand.

III. Once the paw touches your hand, hold it and tell him/her "good". Open your fist and allow the dog to take the treat.

IV. Repeat this for about 5-10 minutes, 2-3 times a day. Your dog will be so willing to offer his/her paw whenever you give the command.

Advice

In case the frequent use of the tricks above doesn't work, try issuing the "shake paw" command and then reach down for her paw. Shake the paw and tell the dog "good" every time you hold the paw. With time, your dog will learn and understand the trick.

Chapter 15: WAVE

This trick is very enjoyable for many dogs and having them wave you good-bye can be exciting. It can be a good way for your dog to impress your visitors when they are leaving and training the trick doesn't take long.

How to do it

I.   If your dog has learned the "shake paw" trick, training the wave trick will be very easy. Waving the paw is normally good when done on top of shaking trick as this sequence makes it very easy for your dog to learn this new trick.

II.   Give your dog a "sit" command and once in this position, give the "shake" instructions. Your dog having learned the shake trick will definitely lift his/her paw intending to shake your hand. Slightly move your hand upwards thus luring your dog to lift his/her paw to reach your hand.

III. Once your dog has lifted his/her paw further upwards, tell him/her "good" and give a treat. Repeat the second step several times until your dog learns how to raise his/her paw a little higher above his/her head.

IV.   Once your dog masters how to put his/her paw up for several times repeatedly, give the "shake" command and once he/she tries reaching for your hand, give the "wave" command or say "hello" while waving your hand gently. Do this again and again preferably 4 times in a day.

V. As your dog starts obeying the "wave" command, try to stop using the "shake" command and build consistency.

VI. Practice giving the "wave" command for 2-3 times, each session taking several minutes in a day. With time, your dog will start waving you or your visitor goodbye or hello as a norm.

Advice

- Start phasing out the treat once your dog has started offering his/her paw on command. You can do this by holding a treat in one hand and once he/she obeys the command, avoid giving him/her the treat in the clasped hand and instead give one from elsewhere.
- Gradually hold your hand out without a treat and if your dog obeys, just pat and praise him/her.
- A treat might be given from time to time as a way of reinforcing the behavior/trick.

Chapter 16: BARK OR SPEAK

Teaching your dog to speak or bark can be a good way of keeping off strangers and funny intruders from your property. It can also help in alerting you of any unwelcome presence within your compound. The "speak" command can be combined with "quiet" command thus training the dog to bark and keep quiet when appropriate.

How to do it

I.   Pick one word to use when giving the bark command. This word should be simple and easy to remember. You can use "talk," "speak" or "bark". Likewise, choose another word to use for "quiet" command. You can choose "quiet," "enough," or "hush'. Don't mix different names for the command though, just pick one and stick with it.

II. In case your dog barks, you should briefly recognize it by checking the cause of the barking. This could be done by moving towards your dog or looking through the door or window. Capture his/her attention by clapping, whistling or using a similar sound.

III. Once the barking stops, speak the command in a firm, audible but upbeat tone while at the same time praising the dog and giving a treat.

IV. To train the "quiet" command, speak the chosen word anytime your dog barks but do not prolong the sessions. The command can be spoken as you stroke the dog and if your dog understands and responds to the instructions, try switching to the "bark" command.

V.   You can strategically plan for a situation that will make your dog to bark such as having someone knock at the door or ring the doorbell. While this is happening, speak the "bark," "speak," or "talk" command in a clear, upbeat tone.

VI.   Once your dog barks 3-4 times in succession, applause by praising "nice bark," or "good speak" while giving a treat. Repeat this process several times until you are sure that your dog has understood the instructions.

VII.   If your dog understands both "bark" and "quiet" commands separately, try to use them together. Create a situation that will cause him/her to bark and then say "speak" and after a few barking, command" "quiet".

Advice

Always give a treat immediately after your dog has obeyed. You should make the treat tasty and if possible, offer your dog one of his/her favorite pieces of food.

Chapter 17: SPINNING

Spinning can be an entertaining trick yet a very simple thing to train your dog. You can train to spin clockwise, counter-clockwise, or alternate between these two directions whenever giving a "spin" command.

How to train

I.   Have a treat in your hand and wave it in front of your dog before giving a "spin" command. Pull the treat towards one side of the dog's head and as he/she turns, keep moving it such that he/she will spin trying to catch a glimpse of the treat. As you continue pulling the treat in circles, your dog's body will spin in the same direction.

II. If your dog follows the treat in a few complete circles, tell her "good" and then let her have the treat.

III. Do this several times every day until your dog masters the trick fully and is able to spin without trouble, and without the treat.

IV. You can also say "spin" and start spinning to see whether your dog will follow suit.

Advice

You can start training your dog to spin in different directions by moving the treat to the left or right. Say "spin right" or "spin left" and move the treat towards that direction. With time, start issuing the commands without a treat if your dog has shown some understanding on how to respond. Practice this every day until your dog can spin without any hand motions.

Chapter 18: ROLL OVER

Teaching your dog the "roll over" trick can be fun and enjoyable. To make it easier, it is important to make sure that your dog understands the "sit" and "lie down" commands to minimize the difficulties associated with the training. Teaching the "roll over" command is not easy and should be done patiently.

How to train

I. Begin by giving your dog the "down" command. Immediately your dog lies down, hold a treat close to his/her nose and then pull it towards his/her shoulders in a way she will follow it and issue the command "roll over". Your dog will start turning his/her head to follow the movements of the treat and this should be followed by pulling the treat further to force him/her to lie on her side. Pull the treat all the way while still holding it close to the nose so that your dog will roll over with his/her legs up. If he/she completes the roll, praise him/her and then give the treat.

II. Try breaking the training sessions into short episodes and follow the step above approximately 6 times for 10 minutes a day.

III. Some dogs can be trained differently by taking the position of a lying dog while she is next to you. Say "roll over" and start rolling in a playful way. If he/she follows your movements, roll a few times as you repeat the command and then try using the treat and try to make your dog roll alone.

Advice

- It might be tough at times to have your dog turn completely. However, you can encourage him/her by giving treats every time he/she turns his/her head in an angle that leaves him/her lying down on her side. Use different treats while trying to encourage your dog to roll over completely.
- As your dog starts rolling over more and more, try phasing out the treats and practice more until he/she masters the moves.

Chapter 19: PLAY DEAD

This is a fun trick to train your dog, especially if you would like to show off to your guests or use your dog in festivals.

How to train

I. Begin by giving your dog the "down" command. Once she is lying down, give a "bang" command while holding your fingers to look like a gun. Point them towards the dog when giving the command.

II. Once you have given the "bang" command, hold a treat next to your dog's nose and then pull it over to his/her side slowly. This will make him/her roll over towards the side of the treat, something that doesn't have to be difficult if the dog understands how to roll over.

III. Once the dog lies on his/her side, say "good" and then give him/her the treat.

IV. Train your dog to assume the lying position for a few minutes and several times each day as you repeat the "bang" command with your "gun fingers" pointing to him/her.

V. Have your dog remain down on his/her side and the more he/she obeys, give praise and a treat. Have him/her lie down for longer moments and as you succeed in this, start withdrawing the treats gradually.

Advice

- If it is hard to have your dog lie down using the above tips, start showing what you want by doing it yourself. You can use the treats as a lure and only give them after he/she remains on the ground lying down for a few seconds. Try increasing the duration of time for which your dog should remain down and playing dead. The more you do it the greater the success.

Chapter 20: BEG

There is nothing as amazing as having your dog sit down to beg you for something. This dog trick is easy for you to train but you should be patient when doing it.

How to train

I. Start by asking your dog to sit down. You should not forget to rehearse all the commands and tricks above. This will help your dog to remember every trick or command and make it a part of his/her life.

II. Once in a sitting position, wave a treat close to his/her nose but hold it firmly before giving the "beg" command.

III. Your dog will try to use his/her mouth to get the treat but raise it higher and higher until it is out of reach with his/her mouth. He/she will next raise his/her paws in a begging position while sitting on hind legs trying to get the treat.

IV. Once in this position, say "good" and then give the treat.

V. You can also place the treat close to his/her right front paw and say "beg". As he/she tries to reach out for the treat, move it further upwards to allow him/her to follow it with the same paw. Hold the treat in an unreachable position and try to keep him/her in that position for a few seconds.

VI.   If he/she accepts to take the begging position, say "good" in an upbeat tone and then give the treat.

VII.   Repeat the process for about 10 minutes a day until your dog understands the command.

Chapter 21: CRAWL

This is an amazing trick to train your dog especially if you have already taken it through the "lay down" trick. To help your dog learn this trick faster, try to make the lessons fun and enjoyable, while at the same time employing positive reinforcement.

How to do it

I. Instruct your dog to lie down while having a few treats nearby. Once the dog lies down, assume the same position but facing him/her.

II. Pat the floor while holding the treat to the ground and motion to the dog as you give the command "crawl". Avoid using other words such as come as this could confuse your dog.

III. In case your dog gets up and starts coming, say "no" in a firm but upbeat voice. Do not try to push your dog down otherwise he/she might think you are punishing her or interpret it for a game. However, if your dog makes an attempt to crawl, say "good" and give a treat.

IV. Gradually increase the crawling distance as your dog manages to crawl for a short distance. It will be good to repeat the word "crawl" with every move your dog makes until she reaches you.

V. As your dog obeys the "crawl" command, gradually phase out the treats.

Chapter 22: JUMP

Jumping can be a difficult trick to train your dog. However, it is one of the best tricks if your dog is able to learn it and results can be achieved if it is done patiently.

How to do it

I. Start by setting up the jumps (obstacles of a certain height) depending with the size of the dog. It is however advisable to start with lower jumps and increase the height with time.

II. Leash your dog and have him/her stand next to you with the jumps in front of you. Start walking fast towards the jumps as you give the command, "jump". You should be holding a treat in your hands and if the dog jumps one hurdle, give him/her a treat before jumping the next.

III. In case the dog hesitates, you can help him/her by lifting her over the hurdles as you repeat the command "jump". Try leading the dog to jump the next hurdle and if he/she does, praise her.

IV. Raise the hurdles higher and repeat the process once more. Once you get a positive response from your dog, remove the leash and have your dog stand at the end of the jumps. Command him/her to stay and walk to the opposite end of the jumps and command him/her to jump.

V.   If he/she obeys the command, wait for him/her at the end of the jumps with a treat. Praise and give the treat. The process of teaching should be done a few times every day to help your dog master the process fully.

Chapter 23: STAND TALL

This command is important not only because it is fun but also helps your dog to develop core strength in its hind legs.

How to do it

I.   Have a treat or a target stick in your hands. The target stick might be ideal if your dog is not easily motivated by food.

II.   Have your dog stand in front of you and directly face each other. Bring the treat or target stick near your dog's nose and slowly lift it higher allowing him/her to try to reach it. At first, your dog will try using its mouth but do not let him/her reach the treat or target stick.

III.   As you raise it higher, give the command "stand tall" and once your dog starts raising its front legs, say "good" and continue raising the treat. Your dog is likely to get back on his/her fours after a few seconds. Give him/her a treat and repeat the process again.

IV.   Repeat the process for 10 minutes at least 5-6 sessions a day. Gradually phase out the treats and praise your dog whenever he/she stands tall.

Chapter 24: TAKE A BOW

This is a great dog trick especially if you want your dog to show off some of the tricks it has learned. It involves your dog leaning forward with his/her elbows and chest to the ground while his/her back end remains raised up.

I. Wiggle a treat at the end of your dog's nose but do not let him/her taste or eat it. Move it away but hold it close to his/her body. Doing this utilizes the treat a lure to cause your dog to bend until his/her elbows touch the ground with the rear end staying up.

II. Hold your dog in that bowed position for some seconds before using the treat as a lure to get her back on his/her feet again.

III. Once your dog has bowed down and stood on his/her feet, praise and give the treat.

IV. Repeat the process several times until your dog is able to understand the trick.

Advice

Some dogs are able to master this trick faster than others and therefore you shouldn't be discouraged if it doesn't happen too soon. Do not push your dog to the ground as this could be interpreted to mean something else other than what you intend to achieve.

Chapter 25: CLOSE DOORS

Teaching your dog this trick can help you relax whenever you want to do absolutely nothing but watch your TV and enjoy your coffee.

How to do it

I. Start by training your dog to touch a specific object such as a playing card taped to the wall, or a ruler, which should be situated somewhere within the house. Once your dog has accepted the "touch" command, praise and give a treat.

II. Once your dog has mastered this, start teaching him/her to go for a given knob or lock on the door. If your dog does this every time you give the command, give him/her a reward and praise.

III. Next will be to start issuing a "close," "door" or "shut" command directing the dog to an open door. Your dog is likely to use her mouth at the beginning followed by the use of front legs. Any attempt to close the door should be appreciated and rewarded.

IV. Practice opening the door 4-5 times within 20 minutes and every time give your dog your chosen cue. Every time your dog closes the door, praise him/her and give a reward. The process of training should be repeated until your dog is familiar with the command and can obey without getting a treat.

Conclusion

Training your dog requires patience and consistency. It is important to always reward your dog for any positive gesture shown towards obeying the commands given, until the art has been mastered fully. However, the most important step towards successful dog training is always to understand how to communicate with your best friend.

Different dogs respond differently to differently commands, treatments and environments. It is therefore important to understand your dog and know what makes him/her happy and easy to please. Do not give all the commands at once but first of all wait for your dog to respond and understand one command and fully obey it before issuing the next one. As with human beings, you should refresh your dog's memory frequently by repeating some of the commands that he/she has already mastered, otherwise he/she could easily forget as you train new tricks.

Training your dog will go a long way in improving his/her behavior and making him/her a joy to spent time with. Do not over exaggerate your expectations or use punishment to vent your anger on your dog if he/she does not respond as desired. Take time to train a single command or trick at a time. With time, you will enjoy amazing results and companionship from your dog. If you can train your dog while still young, the better results you are likely to get. However, do not despair even if your dog is old, all is not lost and great results are still obtainable. Contrary to the saying, old dogs actually can learn new tricks.

Thanks for purchasing this book! If you found it helpful or interesting, I'd really appreciate you taking a moment to leave a review on Amazon.

Made in the USA
San Bernardino, CA
17 March 2017